The Wedding Planner 1

1. Cover the front and back of a spiral bound book.

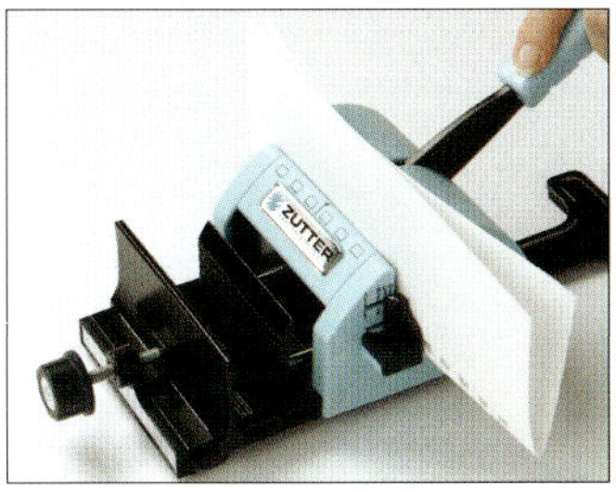

2. Punch holes for the spiral holes with a Zutter tool.

3. Tie ribbon pieces to each coil on the spine.

4. Adhere rhinestones and a label to the cover.

Wedding Planner Book

The bride needs a special notebook to keep up with all the important details for her big day. Choose your favorite themed papers. Recover a spiral bound book or make your own to organize all the "to do lists".

SIZE: 4½" x 8½"

MATERIALS:
4½" x 8½" spiral book (or chipboard, metal spiral and a Zutter tool for making your own book) • Romance theme cardstock and papers (outside covers 5" x 9½", inside covers 3½" x 8¼", 12 papers 3¾" x 8¼") • 8½" x 11" Clear adhesive transparency • Rhinestone designs • Chipboard label • 32 ribbons 4" long • Punches (⅛" square, 3" file tab) • Awl • Adhesive

INSTRUCTIONS:

Covers: Take apart the spiral bound book, spreading coils gently and sliding out all pages and covers (or make your own book). Adhere outside cover papers to front and back covers. Miter corners, fold excess paper to the inside. Re-punch holes for spiral coils using an awl. Adhere inside papers to inside covers. Apply rhinestone designs and adhere chipboard label to the cover. Generate words "wedding planner" on computer and print on adhesive transparency. Trim to fit on label and attach.

Inside Dividers: Punch square holes for spiral coils in 12 papers. Divide the pages of the book between each paper. Punch 12 file tabs. Computer print these words on Clear adhesive transparency: Rings, Dress, Flowers, Music, Church, Minister, Bridesmaids, Groomsmen, Reception, Cake, Favors, Honeymoon. Trim to fit tabs and attach to tabs.

To Finish: Slide pages, dividers, and covers back on spiral coils and press coils closed. Tie ribbon pieces to coils on spine.

Announcing the engagement of
Donna Lynn Morrison
to
Alan Duncan Goss
Wedding set for Saturday,
October twenty-fourth, two thousand and seven
at Mimosa Lane Baptist Church
Mesquite, Texas
Save the Date
Save the Date
June twenty-third,
two thousand and seven
for the wedding of
Kristen Cole
and

Engagement Announcements

2

Announcements are yours in a variety of styles. Add a printed vellum layer over a photo, make a lovely photo card, a monogrammed keepsake card with butterfly and buttons, a lovely book mark or a card that proclaims, "Save the Date!"

Vellum Announcement

SIZE: 4¼" x 5½"

MATERIALS:
Cardstock (4¼" x 5½" White, 4" x 5¼" print) • 4" x 5¼" Cream vellum • 3" x 4" Black & White photo • 6" Peach ribbon ⅜" wide • 1" White flower • Green rhinestone • 4 Copper photo corners • ¼" hole punch • Glue dots • Glue stick

INSTRUCTIONS:
Adhere printed cardstock to White card. Attach photo with photo corners. Print information on vellum. Cut to fit card. Punch 2 holes at top through vellum and card. Thread ribbon through holes from front to back. Cross over ends and bring to front. Adhere rhinestone to flower center and attach flower to ribbon.

Save the Date Photo Card

SIZE: 4¼" x 5½"

MATERIALS:
SEI (4¼" x 5½" glossy print card; 2" x 5½" Blue print cardstock; 2½" x 3" coaster tag; ⅝" x 2" cardstock tab; 6" Yellow ¼" ribbon) • 2" x 2" Black & White photo • 3 Pink brads • *Rubber Soul* 'Save the Date' stamp • *Ranger* (Archival Jet Black inkpad, Glossy Accents) • Awl • The Ultimate! glue • Foam tape • Glue stick

INSTRUCTIONS:
Adhere Blue strip to card. Adhere ribbon along the edge of the strip and trim ends even with card. Poke three holes into card and insert brads. • Stamp "save the date" on tab and apply tab to coaster tag. Adhere photo behind coaster window. Apply Glossy Accents to berries on coaster tag. Let dry. Tape coaster tag to card.

Bookmark Card

SIZE: 3½" x 8"

MATERIALS:
White cardstock (3½" x 8", 3½" x 4¼") *SEI* (Decorative paper:3¼" x 7¾", 3¼" x 4"; 2⅜" x 3⅝" chipboard coaster tags; 2 Blue 5" ribbons ½" wide) • 8½" x 11" Clear adhesive transparency • 6 Clear rhinestones • 4 Silver ⅛" eyelets • Eyelet tools • Glue stick

INSTRUCTIONS:
Adhere decorative papers to White cardstock pieces. Lay smaller White cardstock piece over bottom of larger one to form a pocket. Attach using an eyelet in each corner. Apply rhinestones on top of eyelets and in top corners. Generate words on computer and print on Clear adhesive transparency. Cut to fit over chipboard tag. Run ribbon through the slots in tag and tie with knots. Slip tag into pocket.

Announcement Card

SIZE: 4¼" x 5½"

MATERIALS:
SEI (4¼" x 5½" Aqua card; 2⅛" x 2⅛" Green die cut with butterfly; 2½" x 4¼" Brown lace paper; 1¼" cardstock alphabet sticker) • 4" Blue ⅜" wide ribbon • 7 Blue buttons • 7 Green rhinestones • 1¼" metal rim tag • *Tsukineko* Versamagic inkpads (Sea Breeze, Aloe Vera) • *Ranger* Glossy Accents • Glue stick • Glue dots

INSTRUCTIONS:
Ink card edges with Sea Breeze. Glue lace paper to bottom of card. Ink edges of Green square with Aloe Vera and adhere to card. • Adhere alphabet sticker to metal rim tag. Apply Glossy Accents to letter. Let dry. Knot ribbon in metal tag and adhere to card. • Adhere buttons and rhinestones to card.

Save the Date Card

SIZE: 4¼" x 5½"

MATERIALS:
SEI (4¼" x 5½" pastel print card; Cardstock: 3¼" x 3¼" Aqua, 3½" x 3½" White, 1¼" x 1¼" White; 3" x 3" Peach frame sticker) • *Making Memories* 1" metal ring plaque • 6 Green rhinestones • 2" long ribbons (3 Pink ⅝" wide, 3 White ⅜" wide) • *Rubber Soul* Save the date stamp • *Ranger* Archival Jet Black inkpad • Glue dots • Glue stick • Foam tape

INSTRUCTIONS:
Stamp "Save the Date" on Peach frame. Layer Peach frame, Aqua square and large White square. Adhere metal plaque to small White square and then to center of Peach frame. Tape large White square to card. • Trim ribbon ends into "V's". Adhere White ribbon to Pink with glue dots. Adhere ribbon to card under large White square using glue dots. Apply rhinestones to White ribbon.

3 Shower Invitations

Lingerie Shower Invite

An advantage to making your own invitations is that you can design it to reflect the theme of your party. This Shower card jump-starts the fun and builds anticipation.

SIZE: 4" x 8½"

MATERIALS:

Heidi Grace (Cardstock: 4" x 8½" floral, 2¾" x 7¼" floral, 3" x 7½" Silver, 8½" x 11" White; 2⅜" x 2⅜" stripe paper) • 18" White ⅝" wide ribbon • 6 Pink rhinestones • *Rubber Soul* Lingerie stamp • *Clearsnap* Silver inkpad • *Ranger* (Silver embossing powder, Heat it Craft Tool) • Glue stick • Foam tape

INSTRUCTIONS:

Layer and adhere Floral cardstock, Silver, and Floral. • Computer print invitation on White cardstock. Trim to 2⅜" x 6¾". Emboss image beside words. Apply rhinestones. • Wrap ribbon around stripe paper and tie a bow. Glue to White cardstock. Adhere White cardstock with foam tape.

File Folder Couples Invite

It's not the same old invitation! This File Folder will sure make a splash at the shower.

SIZE: 4¼" x 5½"

MATERIALS:

Heidi Grace (Cardstock: 8½" x 11" Ivory; Double sided Blue floral: 8½" x 11", two 2⅞" x 3⅜"; Flowers: 2 Ivory 2" flocked, 3 Teal 1" flocked, 2 Aqua 1" glittered, 2 plastic 1"; 1½" x 3" Plastic heart; 4 mini brads; 'Celebrate' rub-on) • Paper clip • 2 pieces 4" string • Bone folder • File folder template • Tiny tag template • *Tsukineko* Versamagic Ocean Depth inkpad • Punches (3" file tab, ⅛" hole punch) • The Ultimate! glue • Glue stick • Glue dots

INSTRUCTIONS:

Copy file folder template (page 8) onto double-sided cardstock. Cut out. Score at center and fold in half. • Ink edges of plastic heart, folder and both Blue floral rectangles. Let dry. • Computer print party information so it can be cut into 2 rectangles 2⅝" x 3⅛". Mount words on the Blue rectangles and adhere inside the file folder. • Punch file tab from Ivory cardstock. Fold in half and attach to edge of folder. Trim away excess folder around punched tab. Apply rub-on to tab. • Computer print words "you're invited" and trace tiny tag template over each word. Cut out and punch hole to attach string. Attach 2 Aqua glittered flowers to paper clip using brad and secure brad to clip with glue. Attach 2 Teal flocked flowers with brad, then adhere to back of paper clip flower with a glue dot. Attach paper clip to folder. Adhere tags beneath paper clip. Attach remaining flowers together using brads. Adhere heart and flowers to file folder.

Shower Favors 4

'It's Time' Shower Invite

Handmade invitations are always nice to receive in the mail. This unique design will make your party date more memorable.

SIZE: 5" x 5"

MATERIALS:

Heidi Grace (5" x 5" double-sided print card; Cardstock: 3/4" x 4" floral, 8½" x 11" Ivory; 1" x 5" Borders satin sticker; 2 Brown brads; Flowers: 2 glitter 1¾", Brown plastic 1"; Chipboard clock hands) • *Heidi Swapp* 4" Clear plastic clock • *Tsukineko* Versamagic Jumbo Java inkpad • Awl • Glue stick • Glue dots • Foam tape

INSTRUCTIONS:

Printing: On Ivory cardstock, computer print "it's time..." and "to shower NAME with gifts". Include day, date, time, address, and RSVP phone number. Cut out "it's time" to 5/8" x 1" and trim shower details to 3" x 3½". Ink edges.

Outside: Attach border sticker to card. Ink edge of clock and hands. Let dry. • Poke hole in clock center and card. Insert brad through hands and clock to attach to card. Attach "it's time" to card using foam tape.

Inside: Insert brad through flowers and adhere using glue dots over brad prongs that show from attaching clock. Mount the shower details on Floral rectangle and glue inside card.

Triangle Treat Favor

Just the right size for a specialty chocolate or a tea light candle in your favorite scent, this Triangle Treat Favor is a snap to make.

SIZE: 3" x 3"

MATERIALS:

Cardstock (4" x 6" Floral, 1" x 1½" White) • 10" Brown 3/8" wide ribbon • 2 Silver plastic rings • Silver jump ring • 5 Silver 1/8" eyelets • Tiny tag template • Stamps (*Inky Antics* Triangle Treat template, *American Art Stamp* 'Just a little something') • *Ranger* Archival Jet Black inkpad • Eyelet tools • Bone folder • Ruler • 1/8" hole punch

INSTRUCTIONS:

Stamp triangle treat template on back of floral cardstock in Black ink. Cut out. Score on dotted lines. Set eyelets in 4 sides. Fold up box on lines to form triangle. Thread ribbon through holes to close box. Tie rings in bow. • Trace tiny tag template on White cardstock and cut out. Stamp "Just a little something" on tag using Black ink. Set an eyelet in tag. Attach tag with jump ring to one of the rings.

Take Out Box Favor and Scallop Purse Favor Instructions are continued on pages 8 and 9.

Shower Invitations

Continued from page 6

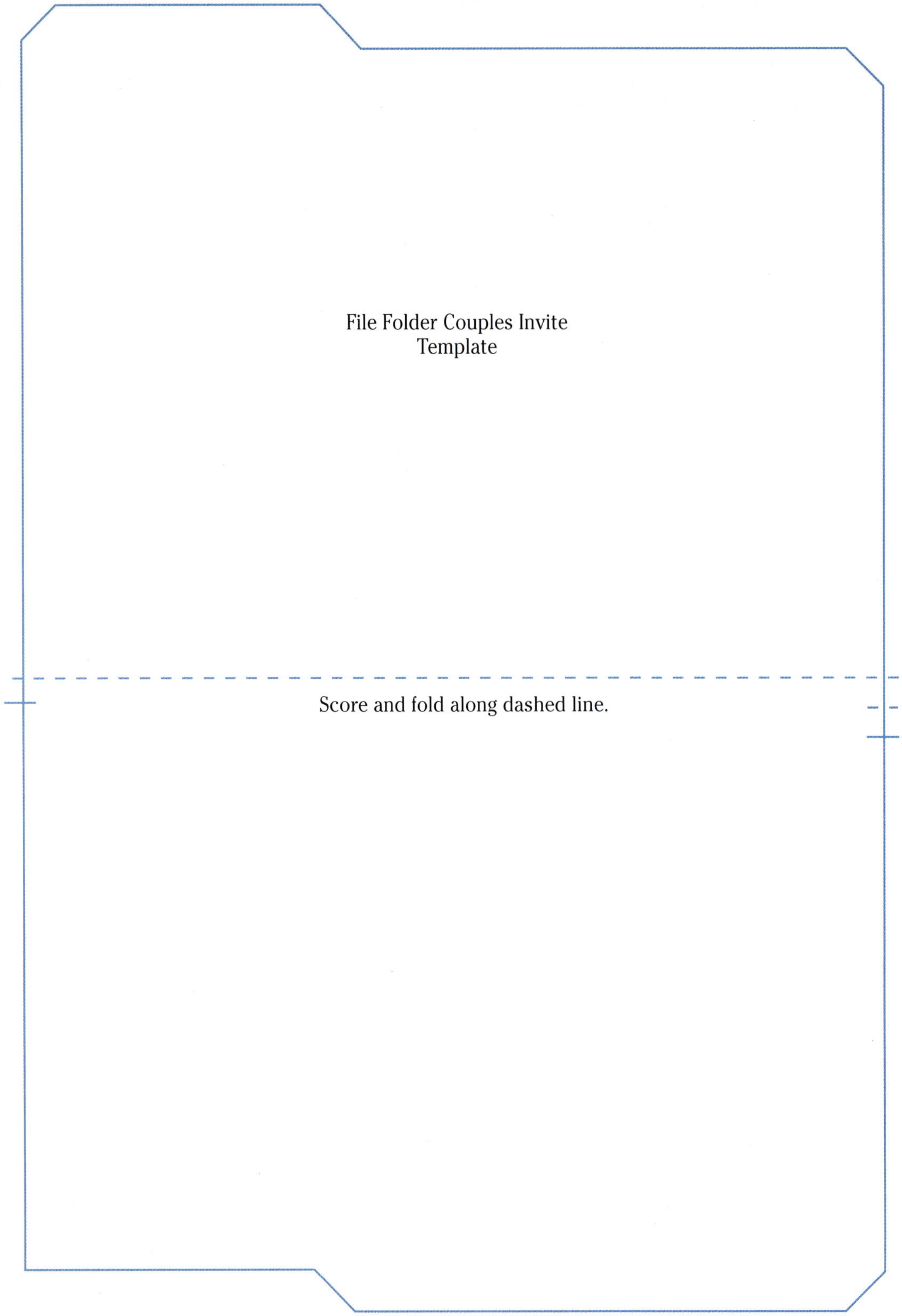

Scallop Purse Favor

Fill this cute purse favor with your favorite candy or surprise everyone with an embroidered handkerchief.

SIZE: 4½" x 5½"

MATERIALS:
Cardstock (12" x 12" Paisley, 1" x 2" White) • *AccuCut* Scallop purse die cut • Chipboard shapes (1⅛" x 2¾" label, 1⅛" circle) • 1¼" metal rim tag • 10" Pink ⅛" wide ribbon • Brads (1 Brown, 2 rhinestone mini, 1 Pink mini) • Flowers (3 small, 1 large) • *American Art Stamp* 'Just a little something' • *Ranger* (Silver embossing powder, Heat it Craft Tool, Jet Black Archival inkpad) • *Clearsnap* Silver inkpad • Awl • Glue dots

INSTRUCTIONS:
Die cut purse from paisley cardstock. Emboss front of label with Silver embossing powder and ink. Attach White cardstock behind label and write name of recipient. Attach label to back of purse using rhinestone brads. Layer 2 small flowers and secure using Pink brad. Adhere to back of purse. • Layer small flower on large one and secure with a Brown brad. Adhere to front of purse. • Fold purse into shape and close using tab. • Stamp "Just a little something" on chipboard circle in Black ink. Adhere circle to metal rim tag. Punch hole in the tag and tie ribbon to handles of purse.

Continued from page 7

Take Out Box Favor

Express your appreciation with a unique handmade thank you. Everyone will know you cared enough to take the time.

SIZE: 2¼" x 2¾" x 2¼" tall

MATERIALS:
Cardstock (12" x 12" Floral, 3" x 4" White) • Take out box template • 10" Pink ⅛" wide ribbon • 2 Silver eyelets • Pink flowers (2 flocked 2", 1 glitter 1") • Metal 'Thank You' charm • Pink rhinestone • Pink mini brad • *Heidi Grace* Flower stamp • *Ranger* (Silver embossing powder, Heat it Craft Tool) • *Clearsnap* Silver inkpad • Ruler • Eyelet tools • Bone folder • Glue dots

INSTRUCTIONS:
Copy box template onto Floral cardstock. Cut out. Score on dotted lines. Set eyelets on sides of box. Thread ribbon ends through eyelets and secure with knot as handle. Layer flowers and secure with a mini brad. Attach thank you charm over brad. Apply rhinestone to hole in charm. Emboss flower image on White cardstock using Silver powder and ink. Cut out and attach behind flowers. Adhere flowers to side of box. Fold up box into shape and secure with glue dots.

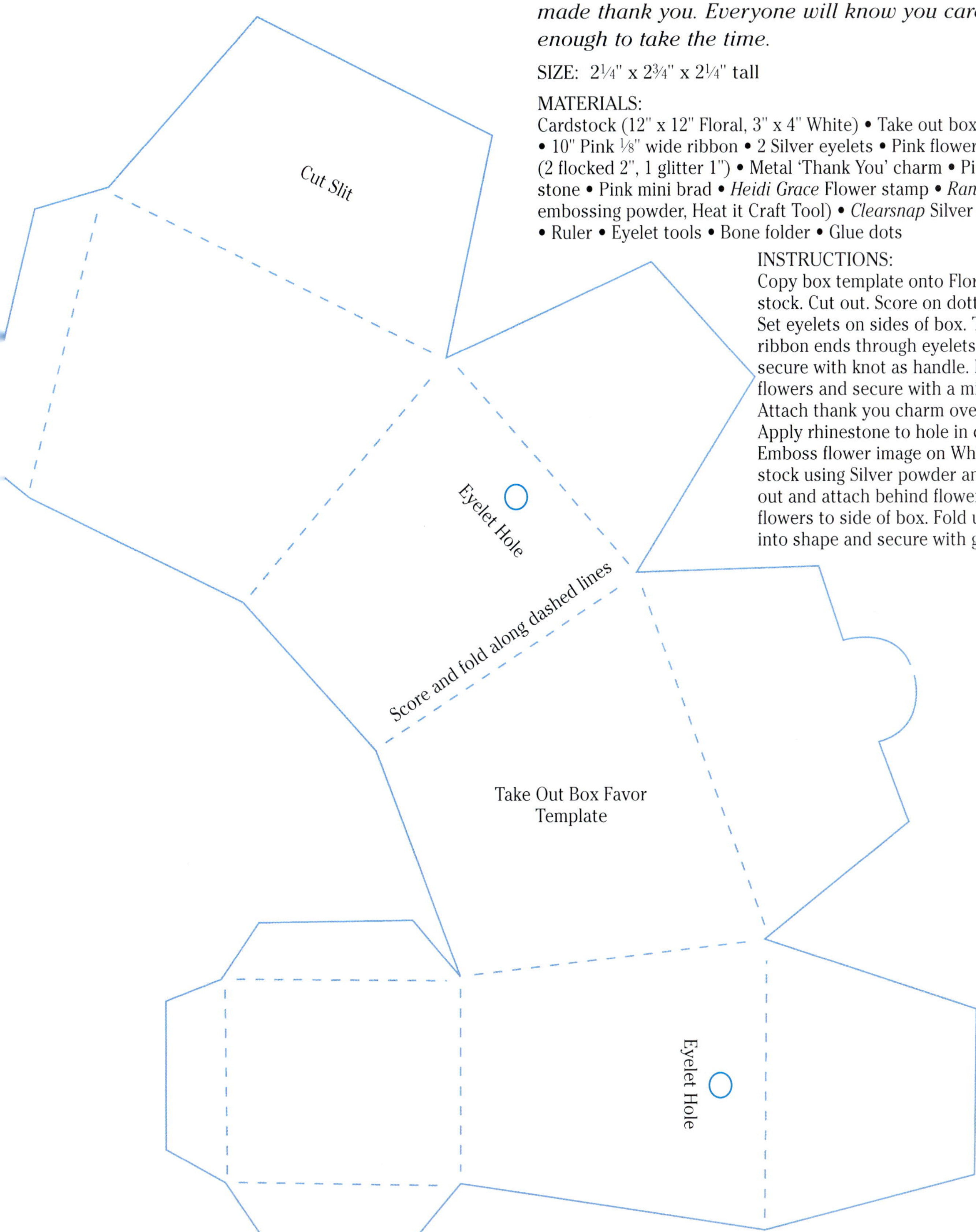

5 Shower Decorations

Dress Centerpiece

This sparkling dress will be the center of attention at the shower.

SIZE: 10" diameter, 11" tall

MATERIALS:

Styrofoam discs (1" x 8", 1" x 10") • Glitter (Teal, Silver) • 1" wide White ribbon (32", 25") • 25 pearl hat pins • 20 gauge wire • White silk leaves • White & Yellow silk flowers • 22 Clear rhinestones • Cardstock (2 Silver 9" x 9", Flourish 6" x 9", Floral 6" x 9") • Dress die cut • 4 chipboard squares 9" x 9" • *Ranger* Lemonade acrylic paint dabber • Wire cutters • Spray glue • The Ultimate! glue

INSTRUCTIONS:

Styrofoam discs: Coat top of both discs with spray glue. Cover small disc with Silver glitter and large one with Teal glitter. Let dry. • Adhere White ribbon around edges of both discs with The Ultimate! glue. Stick pearl hat pins into ribbon around both discs. Glue small disc to top of large one. Let dry.

Dress: Die cut dress from all 4 chipboard pieces. Glue them all together back to back. Paint entire surface including edges with Yellow paint dabber. Let dry. • Die cut dress from 2 Silver cardstock pieces. Glue one to front of chipboard dress sandwich. Cut two 4" wires and bend in half. Attach to back of chipboard dress sandwich. Make sure ends are sticking out from dress. You will use these to stand the dress up in the styrofoam discs. Attach the other Silver dress to the back of chipboard sandwich to cover wires. Die cut skirt portion of dress from Floral cardstock. Trim off the bottom ruffled area. Die cut ruffled portion and bodice of dress from Flourish cardstock. Trim off the hanger are[a]. Glue the bodice and ruffle in plac[e] then layer on the skirt portion. Apply rhinestones to the flower c[en]ters of skirt and where bodice an[d] skirt meet on dress. Adhere a Yellow silk flower to the bodice a[nd] apply a rhinestone to the flower center.

Finish: Stick dress into styrofoam using wires. Stick pearl hat pins i[n] front and back against dress to h[old] secure. Stick silk flowers and leav[es] in styrofoam to decorate front an[d] back of dress.

Add sparkle and cheer to the wedding celebration.

Blessings Book

Invite guests to share the[ir] advice and record good wish[es]. This easy to make bookl[et] will be a treasured keepsak[e]

SIZE: 6" x 6"

MATERIALS:

6" x 6" Floral card • Cardstock (5 Yellow parchments 6" x 11" for pag[es], 3" x 6" Teal for spine, 2¾" x 3¾" Te[al] for title mat, 2½" x 3½" Yellow parc[h]ment for title mat, 8½" x 11" White, 4 White 2" x 4") • 36" White ⅝" wid[e] ribbon • 7 Clear rhinestones • Rub-ons • Chipboard letter • 2 flowers [...] • Brown brad • Word stamps • *Ranger* (Glossy Accents, Archival Jet Black inkpad) • 3" round tab punch • Bone folder • Glue stick

Banner

Add sparkle to the celebration. Display this whimsical banner with the bride and groom's name above the bridal table.

SIZE: each letter 6" wide x 7" tall

MATERIALS FOR 9-FLAG BANNER:

Cardstock (8 Yellow parchment 8½" x 11", 4 coordinated 8" x 12" Prints, 6" x 12" Floral, 6" x 12" Stripe) • Brown ribbons (two 10", eight 8") • *K&Co* Glitter letters • 36 Clear rhinestones • 18 eyelets 3/16" • White crepe paper • *Tsukineko* Versamagic Jumbo Java inkpad • 2 banner templates • Eyelet tools • Sewing machine • Punches (Small flower, 3" round scallop, ¼" circle) • Red line tape • The Ultimate! glue • Glue stick

Note: quantities will vary according to the number of letters in your banner.

INSTRUCTIONS:

Trace Banner Template A on Yellow cardstock and cut out. Ink all edges. Let dry. Trace Banner Template B on 8" x 12" patterned cardstock. Cut out and glue to the Yellow triangles.
• Pleat crepe paper on a sewing machine. Fold paper as you feed it under the sewing machine foot. Trim to fit across top of each triangle. Attach using Red line tape making sure the tape lies along the thread to hold crepe paper together. Trim excess paper off at edges. • Punch scallop circles from 6" x 12" cardstocks. Ink scallop edges. Let dry. Glue to triangles. • Adhere glitter letters to scallops with The Ultimate!. Set eyelets in both top triangle corners. String triangles together using 8" pieces of ribbon. Tie the 10" pieces to the first and last triangle for hanging. • Punch 36 flowers from Teal cardstock. Apply rhinestones to flower centers. Glue flowers to crepe paper and the bottom point of triangles.

Banner Trapezoid Template B

Banner Triangle Template A

NSTRUCTIONS:

Adhere spine piece to card. Computer print "Blessings & Wishes For Name & Name" on White cardstock and cut to 2" x 3". Layer title mats, glue to card. Apply rhinestones to corners of White title and chipboard letter. • Apply Glossy Accents to chipboard letter. Let dry. Adhere to card. • Score all Yellow pages down middle. Stack pages, fold in half. Place inside card. • Tie ribbon in bow around spine to secure pages inside book. Push brad through center of 2 flowers, open prongs, adhere to bow. Punch 4 tabs from White cardstock. Fold tabs in half, adhere to page edges . Stamp words - hugs, laugh, love, wish - on tabs. Adhere rub-ons to decorate the pages.

Heart Shaped Box

The bridesmaid can hang this beautiful heart shaped box on her bedroom door as a keepsake reminder of a wonderful day. Fill the box with jewelry or her favorite candy.

SIZE: 5" x 5"

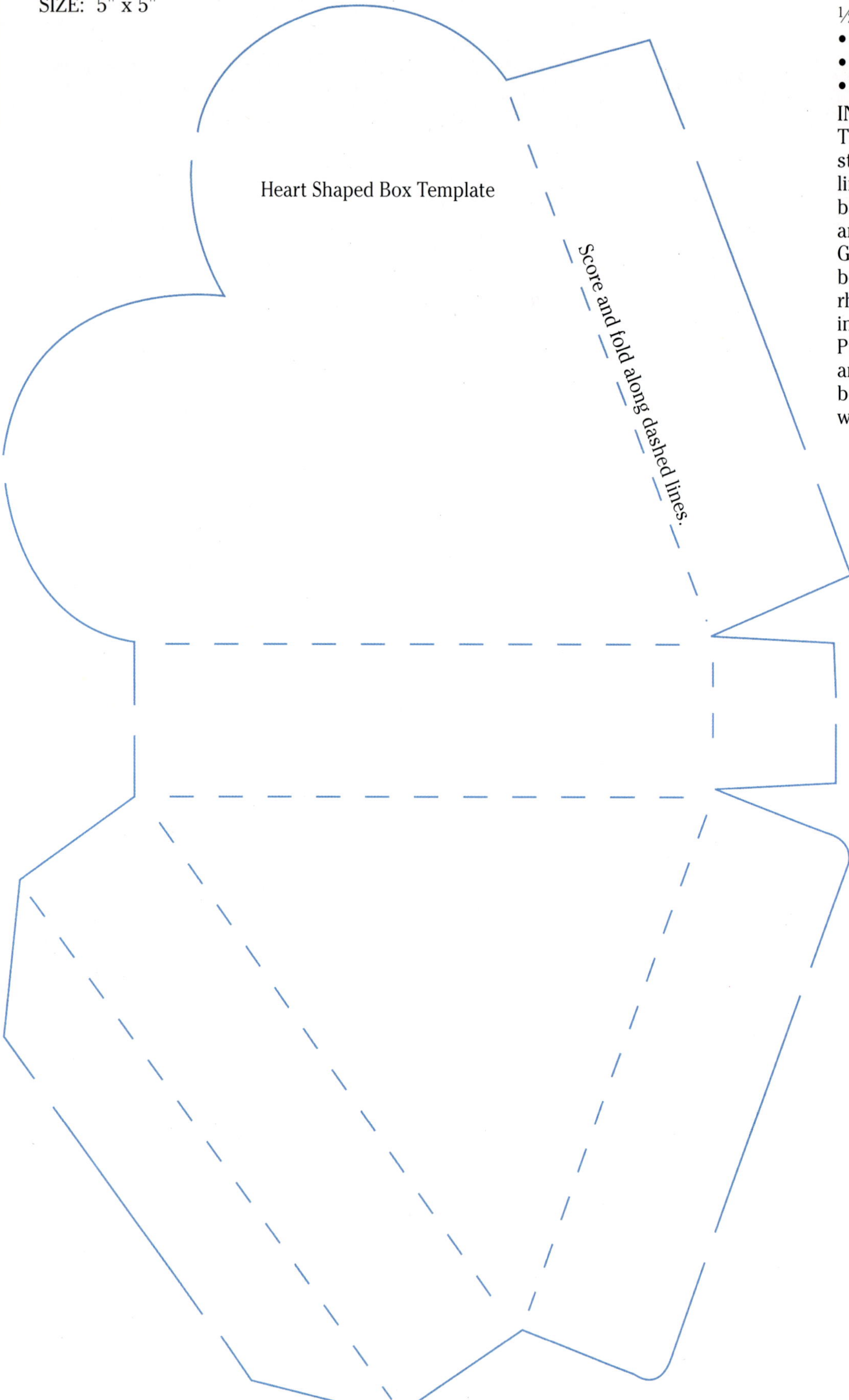

MATERIALS:
6½" x 10" printed cardstock • 10" pleated White crepe paper • 3 flowers 1¼"• 35 Clear rhinestones • 2 White silk 2" leaves • Pearl spray • Ribbon (5" Blue ¼" wide, 18" Aqua ½" wide) • 2 Silver ⅛" eyelets • Eyelet tools • ⅛" hole punch • Heart shaped box template • Red line tape • The Ultimate! glue

INSTRUCTIONS:
Trace and score template on cardstock. Cut out and fold on scored lines. Tape pleated crepe paper to back of heart. Apply rhinestones around heart top on front of box. Glue leaves, pearl spray, Blue ribbon and flowers to box. Apply rhinestones to flower centers. Fold into box shape and tape securely. Punch a hole in each side of box and set eyelets. Thread Aqua ribbon through eyelets and secure with knots.

Gifts for Attendants and Guests 6

Mint Tin

What treasures are hidden within this sparkling tin? A pearl necklace, gold chain, or is it your favorite sweet treat? Personalize each tin for your friends.

SIZE: 2" x 3½"

MATERIALS:
2" x 3½" mint tin • *SEI* (4" x 5" Aqua print cardstock; Flower rub-ons; 1" flower mini coaster; 2" Peach ⅜" wide ribbon) • 11 Blue rhinestones • *Tsukineko* Versamagic Aegean Blue inkpad • *Ranger* Glossy Accents • The Ultimate! glue

INSTRUCTIONS:
Trace around lid and bottom of tin on Aqua cardstock. Cut out. Ink edges. Adhere to lid and inside bottom of box. • Apply rhinestones to lid and center of flower on coaster. Ink edges of coaster. Adhere ribbon and coaster to lid. Apply Glossy Accents to coaster. Let dry.

Remember Me Candle

When this you see, remember me. Simple, elegant, and thoughtful, the Remember Me Candle becomes a treasured reminder of a special day shared with those you love.

SIZE: 3" x 3"

MATERIALS:
3" square glass holder • 2" square candle • 8½" x 11" White cardstock • Ribbons (11" Green, 4" Blue) • 12 tiny flowers in a bunch • Clear rhinestones (9 large, 12 tiny) • ⅛" Silver eyelet • Eyelet tools • ⅛" hole punch • Tiny tag template • The Ultimate! glue • Glue dots

INSTRUCTIONS:
Secure Green ribbon around glass holder with glue dots. Apply 3 large rhinestones to ribbon on sides and back of holder. Apply tiny rhinestones to flower centers. Twist flower stems around pencil to curl. • Computer print "When this you see remember me" on White cardstock. Trace tag template over words and cut out. Punch hole in tag and set eyelet. Tie tag to flowers using Blue ribbon. Adhere flowers to glass holder using The Ultimate!.

Gifts for Guests and Attendants

Decorate something ordinary to make an extraordinary gift.

Monogram Handkerchief

A timeless gift for the groomsman! Stamp a handkerchief with his initial.

SIZE: 18" x 18"

MATERIALS:
18" Men's White handkerchief • *SEI* (Cardstock: 1" x 8" Pink, 2" x 2" Pink, 2" x 2" Aqua stripe; Coaster frame tag; 8" Ivory $\frac{1}{8}$" ribbon) • 36 tiny Clear rhinestones • Stamps (*Wordsworth* Alphabet, *Heidi Grace* Swirl) • *Tsukineko* Versacraft Real Black inkpad • Bird punch • Iron • Glue dots

INSTRUCTIONS:
Stamp letters and swirl on corner of handkerchief using Black ink. Let dry and heat set with iron. Fold handkerchief in pleasing manner and press to set in place. • Wrap 8" cardstock strip around handkerchief and secure with glue dots. Punch bird in center of Aqua stripe square. Attach to back of frame tag using glue dots. Attach Pink square behind frame tag. Slide ribbon through one hole on tag and tie a knot. Wrap ribbon around handkerchief and slide other end through second hole on tag and secure with knot. Apply rhinestones to tag.

Clear Pail Container

Create a decorative keepsake in romantic colors.

SIZE: $4\frac{1}{4}$" diameter x 5" tall

MATERIALS:
Stampendous Clear pint pail • Dove • Cardstock (2 Green flocked 1" x 12", 2 Green flocked 1" x 2", 4" x 4" Green flocked, 4" x 4" White, $3\frac{1}{2}$" White circle) • 3 Pink 2" flowers • Rhinestones (8 large Clear, 4 large Pink, 12 medium Pink, 12 medium Clear) • 32 assorted Pink and White 1" wide ribbons 4" long • Shredded Pink paper • Punches ($3\frac{1}{2}$" circle, 3" scallop circle, $2\frac{1}{2}$" circle) • *Tsukineko* Versamagic Sage inkpad • Red line tape • The Ultimate! glue

INSTRUCTIONS:
Tape 2" Green flocked strips to 12" strips to make 14" long strips. Place one Green flocked strip in bottom inside of pail and the other in the top. Tape ends to secure. • Apply large rhinestones to outside of pail. Punch $3\frac{1}{2}$" White circle, edge with Sage ink. Glue to lid. Punch Green flocked scallop circle. Glue to White circle on lid. Apply medium rhinestones to scallops. Punch $2\frac{1}{2}$" White cardstock circle. Edge with Green ink and glue to scallop circle. • Tie ribbon pieces to handle. Place shredded paper and dove inside the pail. Attach flowers to lid.

Note Cards in a Box

Turn purchased note cards into an exquisite personalized gift with a few simple accents.

SIZE: $3\frac{1}{4}$" x $3\frac{1}{4}$" x $\frac{7}{8}$" tall

MATERIALS:
$3\frac{1}{4}$" x $3\frac{1}{4}$" x $\frac{7}{8}$" tall Clear box • 6 printed cards $2\frac{7}{8}$" x 3" • Cardstock (6 Aqua $2\frac{7}{8}$" x 1", Pink 2" x 6") • 29" Peach ribbon • Vintage rhinestone button • *Wordsworth* Alphabet stamps • *Tsukineko* Versamagic Aloe Vera inkpad • *Ranger* Stardust Stickles, Archival Jet Black inkpad) • Bird punch • The Ultimate! glue • Glue stick

INSTRUCTIONS:
Adhere Aqua strips to cards. Ink all card edges with Aloe Vera. Let dry. Punch 6 Pink birds and adhere to cards. Stamp letter on card in Black ink. Let dry. Apply stickles over letters. Let dry. • Place cards in box and tie ribbon around securing with knot. Glue button on knot with The Ultimate!.

Out of Town Guest Gift Bag

Many times you will have guests from out of town attend the wedding. Welcome them with a gift bag waiting in their hotel room filled with chocolate and bath products.

SIZE: 4" x 8" x 11" tall

MATERIALS:
SEI (Cardstock: 8" x 11" glossy Pastel, 3" x 3" Blue, 4" x 4" Pink, 1" x 8" White print; $2\frac{1}{4}$" round die cut tag; $1\frac{1}{4}$" alphabet sticker) • 6" ribbon $\frac{3}{8}$" wide • $1\frac{1}{4}$" paper flower • 3 Yellow $\frac{1}{2}$" silk flowers • 2" White silk leaf • Pearl spray • 29 Clear rhinestones • *Tsukineko* Versamagic Aloe Vera inkpad • *AccuCut* Bag topper die cut • Punches (3" scallop circle, $2\frac{1}{2}$" circle) • *Ranger* Glossy Accents • The Ultimate! glue • Glue stick • Foam tape

INSTRUCTIONS:
Die cut topper from glossy cardstock. Glue 1" x 8" strip to the topper. Trim ends even at edges. • Glue leaf, pearl spray and flowers to topper using The Ultimate!. Apply rhinestone to paper flower center. • Punch scallop circle from Pink cardstock and small circle from Blue cardstock. Edge both with Aloe Vera ink. Stack circles and glue in place. Apply alphabet sticker to metal rim tag. Attach tag to punched circle using foam tape. Apply Glossy Accents to letter. Let dry. Apply rhinestones to scallops and cardstock strip. Slip topper over handles of gift bag. • Write name on die cut tag. Tie tag to the bag handles with ribbon.

7 Wedding Invitations

Hugs and kisses from the bride and groom. These elegant invitations hold sweet memories of a special day. For an entertaining change, try these uniquely decorated and shaped invitations.

Wedding Dress Invitation

This is a simple whimsical invitation. Generate your wording on the computer and attach to the inside for an enchanting finish.

SIZE: 4¼" x 5½"

MATERIALS:

4¼" x 5½" wedding card • Cardstock (4" x 5" glitter, 1½" x 5½" White for spine) • 6" x 6" White tulle • Rub-ons • 2 flowers • 4 rhinestones • 4" Blue velvet ribbon • *My Sentiments Exactly* Dress stamp • *Ranger* Archival Jet Black inkpad • Bone folder • Foam tape • Red line tape • Glue dots • Glue stick

INSTRUCTIONS:

Score White cardstock down center. Glue over spine of card. Apply rub-ons to White cardstock and corner of card. Apply rhinestones to rub-ons on White cardstock. • Stamp dress on back of glitter cardstock. Cut out. Gather tulle at one end and attach to waist portion of dress using Red line tape. Wrap ribbon around waist and secure with glue dots. Attach flowers to ribbon. Apply rhinestone to center of flower. Adhere dress to card with foam tape.

True Happiness Invitation

Begin the celebration of the most significant day of your life with a truly beautiful handmade invitation.

SIZE: $4\frac{1}{4}$" x $5\frac{1}{2}$"

MATERIALS:
$4\frac{1}{4}$" x $5\frac{1}{2}$" White card • *K&Co* (Cardstock: $3\frac{1}{2}$" x $4\frac{3}{4}$" Pink, 4" x 4" Green stripe; $4\frac{1}{4}$" Green swirl $\frac{1}{2}$" wide ribbon; True happiness sticker) • 23 Clear rhinestones • *Tsukineko* Versamagic inkpads (Sage, Pixie Dust) • 3" scallop oval punch • The Ultimate! glue • Foam tape • Glue stick

INSTRUCTIONS:
Edge Pink cardstock with Pixie Dust ink. Glue to card. Glue ribbon in place. Punch scallop oval from Green stripe cardstock. Edge with Sage ink. Tape over ribbon. Apply sticker to scallop oval. Adhere rhinestone to "i" in happiness on sticker. Apply other rhinestones at ends of ribbon and corners of Pink cardstock.

Tag Folio Invitation

Floral papers lend a touch of Victorian romance and refinement to this invitation.

SIZE: $4\frac{1}{2}$" x $5\frac{1}{2}$"

MATERIALS:
Cardstock (6" x $9\frac{1}{2}$" Blue floral, $8\frac{1}{2}$" x 11" Ivory) • Paper flowers (3 large, 1 medium, 2 small) • Ribbons (8" Plum $\frac{3}{8}$" wide, $3\frac{1}{4}$" Pink velvet $\frac{1}{2}$" wide) • Pearl hat pin • Silver heart charm • 2 Clear rhinestones • *Autumn Leaves* Swirl stamp • *Tsukineko* Versamagic inkpad (Perfect Plumeria, Pixie Dust) • Bone folder • $1\frac{3}{8}$" circle punch • Folio template • Stapler • The Ultimate! glue

INSTRUCTIONS:
Folio: Copy folio template onto Blue floral cardstock. Score and cut out. Fold left side then right over left and glue in place. Fold up bottom and adhere. • Slide heart charm on pin and stick into Pink velvet ribbon. Glue to front of folio. Glue 3 large flowers together and top with small paper flower. Secure rhinestone in center of flower. Glue flowers to ribbon. Use circle punch on top front of folio.
Tag insert: Computer print invitation on Ivory cardstock. Trim to $4\frac{1}{4}$" x $5\frac{1}{2}$" size. Stamp swirls in Pink ink. Ink edges with Plum ink. Staple Plum ribbon as tassel at top of invitation. Glue medium flower over staples then small one on top. Apply rhinestone to center of flower.

Score and fold along dashed lines.

Tag Folio Template

Classy, pretty and sweet! Your guests will enjoy these attractive invitations.

Wedding Invitations

Send a beautiful invitation ... inside and out.

Together Forever Invitation

Clean, simple, classic! Be sure to mail your invitations four to six weeks before the big day.

SIZE: 5¾" x 5¾"

MATERIALS:
Cardstock (5¾" x 14" Ivory, 4¼" x 4¼" Blue, *K&Co* Lace print: 5" x 5", 8½" x 11") • 21 Green rhinestones • 6" Blue ribbon • *K&Co* Together forever sticker • 1⅜" circle punch • *Tsukineko* Versamagic Sage inkpad • *US ArtQuest* puff static pouch • Glue stick • Glue dots

INSTRUCTIONS:
Score Ivory cardstock on the 14" long side at 2⅜", 8¼" and 12". Fold on scored lines to make folio. At the 12" folded piece, punch a circle in the center. Apply glue dots on the sides to make a pocket. Apply 13 rhinestones around punched circle. • Ink the edges of the 5" Lace cardstock. Computer print invitation, response and reception cards on the 8½" x 11" Lace cardstock. Trim the invitation to 4⅛" x 4⅛", the response card to 3" x 5", and the reception card to 2½" x 5". Ink all edges. • Layer and glue to center section of folio: 5" Lace, Blue square, printed Lace. Apply 4 rhinestones to corners. Slide response and reception cards into pocket. • Fold ribbon in half making a loop. Attach to back of sticker. Tap the puff static pouch on the back of the sticker to make the adhesive not sticky. Close folio and attach ribbon and sticker to outside using glue dots. Apply remaining rhinestones to folio.

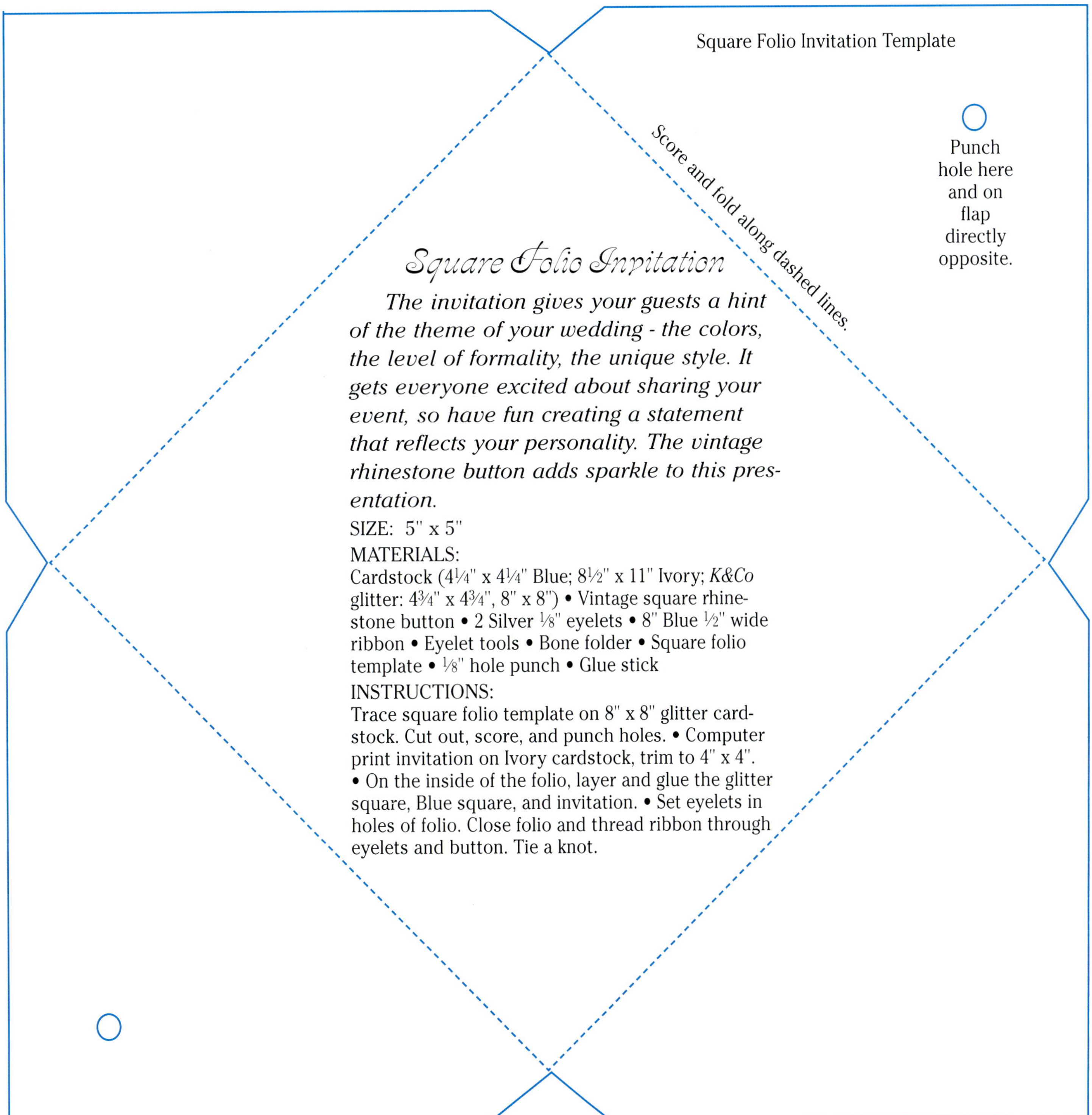

Square Folio Invitation

The invitation gives your guests a hint of the theme of your wedding - the colors, the level of formality, the unique style. It gets everyone excited about sharing your event, so have fun creating a statement that reflects your personality. The vintage rhinestone button adds sparkle to this presentation.

SIZE: 5" x 5"

MATERIALS:
Cardstock (4¼" x 4¼" Blue; 8½" x 11" Ivory; *K&Co* glitter: 4¾" x 4¾", 8" x 8") • Vintage square rhinestone button • 2 Silver ⅛" eyelets • 8" Blue ½" wide ribbon • Eyelet tools • Bone folder • Square folio template • ⅛" hole punch • Glue stick

INSTRUCTIONS:
Trace square folio template on 8" x 8" glitter cardstock. Cut out, score, and punch holes. • Computer print invitation on Ivory cardstock, trim to 4" x 4". • On the inside of the folio, layer and glue the glitter square, Blue square, and invitation. • Set eyelets in holes of folio. Close folio and thread ribbon through eyelets and button. Tie a knot.

8 for the Bride & Groom

Scrapbook

Add small touches to a scrapbook for a beautiful gift that will be appreciated for years to come.

SIZE: 8¾" x 9¾"

MATERIALS:
8¾" x 9¾" book • Cardstock (⅝" x 1¼" Ivory, ⅞" x 1½" Tan) • 8½" x 11" Clear adhesive transparency • Love rhinestone word • 12 Clear rhinestones • *Tsukineko* Versamagic Wheat inkpad • Adhesive

INSTRUCTIONS:
Apply rhinestones to ribbon on book cover. Adhere love rhinestone word to corner of book. Computer print bride and groom names and date on Clear adhesive transparency. Cut to fit Ivory cardstock. Adhere to Tan mat and adhere to book. Apply rhinestones around the names.

Guest Book Pen

An elegantly decorated pen.

SIZE: 2" x 2½" x 8" tall

MATERIALS:
Pen with acrylic base • 8" of Blue-Brown ⅛" ribbon • ½" Blue paper flower • 5 rhinestones • Glue dots

INSTRUCTIONS:
Apply rhinestones to top corners of base and flower center. Tie ribbon on end of pen in bow. Adhere flower to center of bow using a glue dot.

Guest Book

Simple and elegant, a treasured keepsake for the happy couple.

SIZE: 7" x 9"

MATERIALS:
7" x 9" guest book • 45" Blue-Brown ⅛" wide ribbon • 11 Blue rhinestones • Blue ½" paper flower • Glue dots

INSTRUCTIONS:
Apply rhinestones to book cover and center of flower. Tie ribbon around front cover near spine in a bow. Attach flower to bow center using a glue dot.

DVD Cover

The video of your wedding deserves a cover as special as the memory.

SIZE: 5¼" x 7½"

MATERIALS:
5¼" x 7½" blank DVD case • Cardstock (Ivory: 7½" x 10½", 2" x 4¼", 1⅛" x 2½"; Black: 2½" x 10½", 1½" x 3") • 8½" x 11" Clear adhesive transparency • *Tsukineko* Versamagic Wheat inkpad • Adhesive

INSTRUCTIONS:
Ink the edges of the 7½" x 10½" Ivory cover and adhere the 10½" Black strip. Adhere large Ivory mat, Black mat, and small Ivory mat to cover. • Computer print bride and groom names and date on Clear adhesive transparency. Trim to fit title mats. Slide cover into DVD case.

Photo Coasters

After the wedding there are all kinds of items you will want to keep. These coasters provide an interesting forum for displaying your very favorite wedding memories.

SIZE: coaster: 3½" x 3½", stand: 1½" x 4½" x 3½" tall

MATERIALS:
4 glass coasters 3½" x 3½" • Stand • 4 photos

INSTRUCTIONS:
Cut photos to fit coaster. Slide photo in plastic sleeve that comes with coasters. Slide this into coaster.

For the Bride & Groom

Make any frame that coordinates with the wedding colors for a wonderful keepsake or lovely gift.

Scrapbook pages are another way to display your photos. Frame them or attach them to canvas to display them. Decorative papers create a frame as wonderful as the subject and the photo cube, decorative mats and crystal embellishments accentuate the most important day in your life.

'Memories' Scrapbook Page

SIZE: 9" x 9"

MATERIALS:
4" x 6" photo • Cardstock (9" x 9" Brown background, 7½" x 7½" Ivory stripe mat, 5" x 7" Brown mat, 4½" x 6½" Ivory mat) • Journaling spot • 3 flowers • 3 Clear rhinestones • 4 Black photo corners • Black marker • Adhesive

INSTRUCTIONS:
Adhere mats and photo to background. Attach photo using corners. Write "bliss" on journaling spot. Attach to layout. Apply rhinestones to flower centers. Adhere flowers to page.

Nostalgic Frame

SIZE: 8" x 8"

MATERIALS:
8" x 8" wooden frame • 3 different Ivory cardstocks (4½" x 8", 1½" x 8", 3½" x 8") • 120 Clear tiny rhinestones • Rub-ons • 2⅜" Ribbon (2 Ivory ⅜" wide, 2 Gold ⅛" wide) • *Tsukineko* Versamagic Wheat inkpad • Black acrylic paint • Paintbrush • Craft knife • Cutting mat • Adhesive

INSTRUCTIONS:
Paint frame Black. Let dry. • Ink edges of cardstocks. Let dry. Adhere cardstock to frame. Cut out window. Ink edge around the window. Cover cardstock intersections with ribbon. Apply rhinestones around window. Adhere rub-ons.

Turn the traditional wedding photo into a uniquely personal memory with rhinestones and name plate. Encourage the bridal party to sign this frame.

Photo Cube

SIZE: 3½" x 3½"

MATERIALS:

Making Memories (3½" photo cube; Cardstock: 6 Ivory 3½" x 3½", 4 Black 3" x 3½", 1 Black 4" x 4"; 16 Black photo corners; Stickers: 'Together', 'Wedding' circle; Rub-ons) • Clear rhinestones (12 medium, 72 tiny) • 3" scallop circle punch • Adhesive

INSTRUCTIONS:

Prep: Adhere Ivory cardstock to all sides. Adhere 4 Black mats to the sides.
Top: Punch scallop circle from Black cardstock. Attach sticker to punched scallop circle. Adhere to top of cube. Apply rhinestones to dots on sticker.
Sides: Trim 3 photos to 2½" x 2½". Adhere photos to cube using photo corners. Apply stickers, rub-ons, and rhinestones. • Trim remaining photo to 2½" x 2¾". • Attach photo using photo corners. Apply rhinestones to corners.

Autograph Photo frame

SIZE: 12" x 15"

MATERIALS:

10" x 13" frame • 8" x 10" photo • Cardstock (1¼" x 2½" Black, 1" x 2⅛" Ivory) • ⅜" x 5⅛" rhinestone border • 4 Clear rhinestones • Clear adhesive transparency • Glue stick

INSTRUCTIONS:

Place photo behind mat. Apply rhinestone border beside window on mat. • Print bride and groom names, date on Clear adhesive transparency. Cut to fit on Ivory cardstock, adhere to Black cardstock. Adhere Black cardstock below window. Apply rhinestones to mat.

9 Wedding Accessories

Ring Pillow

SIZE: 9" x 9"

MATERIALS:
White satin pillow • Clear rhinestones (19 large, 9 tiny) • 10" Blue 1/8" wide ribbon • Assorted silk flowers • Hot glue gun

INSTRUCTIONS:
Hot glue ribbon to center of pillow. Hot glue flowers over ribbon. Apply large rhinestones around pillow where lace is attached. Apply tiny rhinestones to pillow top around flowers.

Flower Girl Metal Pail

SIZE: 5½" diameter x 9" tall

MATERIALS:
5" metal pail • Ribbons (2 Blue 14" x 3/8" wide; 20 assorted 6" x ½" wide) • 4 Pink 2" diameter silk flowers • Spray of small silk flowers to glue around top of bucket • 4 Clear rhinestones • Assorted White silk flower petals to fill bucket • White bow with pearl heart embellishment • *Ranger* Willow acrylic paint dabber • Hot glue gun • Spray sealer

INSTRUCTIONS:
Paint pail using Willow acrylic dabber. Let dry. Spray with sealer. Let dry. • Hot glue Blue ribbons around bottom and top edges of pail. Hot glue silk flowers around top edge. Tie 6" pieces of ribbon in knots around wire handle. Trim ends at an angle. • Hot glue bow with heart on front of pail. Apply rhinestones in large flower centers.

Garter

SIZE: 12"

MATERIALS:
White lace garter • 8" of Blue ¼" ribbon • Blue ½" paper flower • 2 pearl sprays • Clear rhinestone • Hot glue gun

INSTRUCTIONS:
Attach the pearl sprays to the garter using hot glue. Tie the ribbon into a bow. Attach the bow over the pearl sprays. Apply rhinestone to flower center and adhere flower to bow using hot glue.

Every detail of your wedding day is important. The ring bearer pillow complements the bridal party accessories with matching flowers and sparkling rhinestones. Delicate flowers and ribbon make a unique flower pail, while add-on pearl sprays, ribbon and rhinestones pop this bride's garter.

Rehearsal Bouquet

Use bows from shower gifts to make this bouquet to be used at the wedding rehearsal. Just add flowers.

SIZE: 11" diameter

MATERIALS:
9" satin bouquet holder • Bows from shower gifts • Flowers (Silk, Paper) • 3" Green satin ribbon • Silver 20 gauge wire • Wire cutter • Floral tape • Hot glue gun

INSTRUCTIONS:
Cut a 20" piece of wire for each bow. Fold in half and thread through center of bow. Twist to secure. Start with largest bow, thread wire through bouquet holder. Place in center. Continue to thread in other bows to make ball shape. Secure wires together with florist tape at back of bouquet holder. If needed, attach wire to flowers with tape, then thread through holder. Or glue flowers on bows using hot glue. When all flowers are in place, use florist tape to secure any loose wires. Wrap Green ribbon around tape to finish the handle, securing the end with hot glue.

Add cheer and good will.

Table Centerpiece

Very pretty! Create a unique centerpiece for the bridal table that becomes a pretty keepsake later.

SIZE: 7" x 7" x 16" tall

MATERIALS:

Metal bird cage • Bride/groom centerpiece • Dove • 6 feet White 3" wide tulle • 6 feet of 1/8" wide ribbon (Blue, Blue-Brown) • 6 White paper roses • Blue silk flowers • 3" x 4" pearl initial • 2 Blue rhinestones • Wire • Wire cutters • Hot glue gun • Red line tape

INSTRUCTIONS:

Attach bride and groom in cage using Red line tape. Hot glue flowers around them. • Apply rhinestones to dove's eyes. Attach dove to flowers. Close cage. • Tie pearl initial on top of cage. Tie ribbons and tulle into a bow and secure with wire. Attach to top of cage with wire. Glue flowers to bow center. Glue butterfly to back of bow to hide wire.

Topiary Place Card Holder

SIZE: 4" diameter x 9" tall

MATERIALS:

3" styrofoam ball • 2½" terra cotta pot • 30 Blue 2" diameter silk flowers • 21 White ½" diameter silk roses • 18" Blue ribbon • 8" White doily • *Tsukineko* Versamagic Sea Breeze inkpad • 2" x 3" die cut tag • 8½" x 11" White cardstock • 8" wire 20 gauge • Paintbrush • Gesso • Wire cutter • Round-nose pliers • Hot glue gun • Glue dots

INSTRUCTIONS:

Cover styrofoam ball and terra cotta pot with gesso. Let dry.
• Hot glue ball to inside of pot.
• Hot glue Blue flowers covering ball. Hot glue roses around edge of pot to hide. Wrap pot with doily. Tie ribbon in bow around doily. Secure with glue dots if needed.
• Roll a spiral in one end of wire using Round-nose pliers. Stick other end into top of ball. Print guest name and table number on White cardstock. Trim to fit tag and ink edges. Adhere to tag. Place tag in spiral.

Accessories for the Reception

10

Help guests find their place at the table with place card holders that match your wedding theme... a unique memory for guests to take home.

Ceramic Place Card Holder

Classic white coordinates with any wedding color making this Place Card holder an excellent choice for a formal theme.

SIZE: 2" x 4"

MATERIALS:
2" x 4" ceramic place card holder • Cardstock (1" x 2¼" Blue, 1¼" x 2½" Brown, 8½" x 11" White) • 2 Blue rhinestones • Blue swirl rub-on • *Tsukineko* Versamagic Sea Breeze inkpad • Adhesive

INSTRUCTIONS:
Apply Blue rhinestones to flowers on ceramic holder. Apply rub-on to center of ceramic holder. • Adhere Blue mat to Brown cardstock. • Computer print guest name on White cardstock, trim to ¾" x 2" and ink the edges. Adhere to Blue mat. Adhere name to ceramic holder.

Silver Frame Place Card Holder

Make your guest feel extra special by presenting their name in a sparkling frame.

SIZE: 2½" x 3½"

MATERIALS:
2½" x 3½" Silver frame • 8½" x 11" White cardstock • Blue ½" paper flower • 9 Blue rhinestones • Glue dots

INSTRUCTIONS:
Computer print guest name and table number on White cardstock. Trim to 2" x 3" and place inside frame behind glass. Adhere flower to glass. Apply rhinestones to flower center and frame edges.

Crown on a Tent Place Card Holder

Create an inviting place setting fit for royalty with this Crown Tent Place Card holder.

SIZE: 3½" x 4½"

MATERIALS:
Cardstock (4½" x 7" Brown, 2" x 3" Brown, 2¾" x 3⅞" Blue mat, 8½" x 11" White) • 7 Blue rhinestones • Crown sticker • Ruler • Bone folder • Adhesive

INSTRUCTIONS:
Score 4½" x 7" Brown cardstock and fold to 3½" x 4½". Adhere Blue mat. • Computer print guest name and table number on White cardstock and trim to 2½" x 3⅜". Adhere to Blue mat. Apply crown sticker to White cardstock. Affix rhinestones to crown and corners of Blue mat. • Score 2" x 3" brocade cardstock ½" on each end of long side for easel tabs. Fold on lines. Adhere one tab to inside center front, even at the edge. Adhere other tab to center inside back.

for the Reception

If you want to specify seating assignments, make elegant table number markers that complement the theme and style of the wedding.

Star Table Number

If your reception requires specified seating assignments, this whimsical star is a pretty way to identify the table number. Place it in a plant or vase of flowers for a lovely centerpiece.

SIZE: 4" x 12"

MATERIALS:

3¾" x 3¾" wooden star on stick • 4" x 4" Brown print cardstock • 1¾" die cut circle tag • 6" Blue ½" wide ribbon • 38 Clear rhinestones • Number stamp • *Ranger* Archival Jet Black inkpad • *Tsukineko* Versamagic inkpads (Jumbo Java, Sea Breeze) • Brown acrylic paint • Paintbrush • Adhesive

INSTRUCTIONS:

Trace star on back of Brown print cardstock. Cut out. Paint star and stick Brown. Let dry. Adhere cardstock to wood star. Edge star using Jumbo Java ink pad. Ink edges of tag with Sea Breeze. Stamp number on center of tag in Black ink. Apply rhinestones to circle on tag. Adhere tag to star center. Tie ribbon on stick.

Ceramic Table Number

Add embellishments to this ceramic easel for a one of a kind table number.

SIZE: 6" x 7¾"

MATERIALS:

6" x 7¾" ceramic easel • Cardstock (3½" x 3½" Brown, 3¼" x 3¼" Blue, 8½" x 11" White) • 4 Blue ½" paper flowers • 4 Blue rhinestones • Cake rub-on • Adhesive

INSTRUCTIONS:

Apply rub-on to easel. Adhere flowers to easel. Adhere rhinestones to flower centers. Layer Blue cardstock over Brown. Computer print "Table" and number on White cardstock. Trim to 2¾" x 2¾" and adhere to Blue mat. Adhere cardstock to easel.

Personalized Confetti

Letter punches create personalized confetti to sprinkle on the reception tables. Include flowers for a whimsical feel.

SIZE: ½" - 1½"

MATERIALS:

8½" x 11" Brown cardstock • Alphabet punch • Paper flowers • Rhinestones

INSTRUCTIONS:

Punch first name of bride and groom from Brown cardstock as confetti. Apply rhinestones to flower center. Sprinkle all on reception tables.

Triangle Table Marker

A sparkling butterfly alights each table number for a dazzling enhancement to your decor.

SIZE: 3½" x 8½"

MATERIALS:

8½" x 11" Blue cardstock • 2⅛" x 3¾" die cut tag • 2½" x 3⅜" White butterfly • 4 Blue rhinestones • *Technique Tuesday* stamps (Alphabets, Numbers) • *Tsukineko* Versamagic Sea Breeze inkpad • *Ranger* Archival Jet Black inkpad • Bone folder • Adhesive

INSTRUCTIONS:

Score Blue cardstock on long side at ½", 4⅛" and 8". Stamp "table" and number on die cut tag and two outside panels of cardstock in Black ink. Adhere die cut tag to middle panel. Fold on scored lines and secure in triangle shape using adhesive on the tab. Ink all edges. Apply rhinestones to butterfly and attach to middle panel.

Wedding Camera

Encourage guests to capture candid memories at the reception with these disposable cameras.

SIZE: 1" x 4" x 2" tall

MATERIALS:

Camera • Cardstock (7½" x 7½" Blue, 8½ " x 11" White) • Rub-ons • 10 Blue rhinestones • *Tsukineko* Versamagic Jumbo Java inkpad • Red line tape

INSTRUCTIONS:

Carefully remove the wrapper (box) from the camera to use as a template. Trace around wrapper on Blue cardstock. Cut out and score. Wrap around camera to see where rub-ons can go. Apply rub-ons. Secure cardstock around camera using Red line tape. • Computer print bride and groom names and wedding date on White cardstock. Trim to fit on camera. Ink edges and adhere to camera. • Apply rhinestones.

Create a special setting for the table.

Accessories for the Reception

Decorate for the special occasion dinner or reception. Cake toppers and a pretty menu add to the festivities.

Menu

An elegant meal deserves an elegant menu. This attractive presentation is quite simple to construct.

SIZE: 6" x 10⅜"

MATERIALS:

Cardstock (6" x 10⅜" Brown floral, 4" x 8¼" Blue mat, Ivory: 8½" x 11", 2" x 6", 2" x 3") • 3 Blue ½" paper flowers • 3 Clear rhinestones • 4 Blue photo corners • Bone folder • *Ranger* Glossy Accents • Glue stick

INSTRUCTIONS:

Menu: Print menu on Ivory cardstock and cut to 3¾" x 8". Adhere Blue mat and menu to Brown floral background. • Affix photo corners and apply Glossy Accents to them. Let dry. • Attach flowers and apply rhinestones to centers.

Easel: Score the 2" x 6" Ivory strip ½" from one end to make a tab. Glue tab to the center back of menu 5½" from the bottom. Un-scored end should be even with bottom of menu. Score the 2" x 3" Ivory strip ½" from each end to make tabs. Glue one tab to bottom of the long piece already attached and the other tab to the bottom of the menu.

Whimsical Cake Topper

When tastes run toward the eclectic and lighthearted, this cake topper is a favorite.

SIZE: 3½" wide x 6" tall

MATERIALS:

2 Blue cardstock squares 3½" x 3½" • Chipboard (3½" x 3½" square, 1" x 1¼" heart) • Blue rhinestones (7 medium, 18 small) • 1½" x 2½" Silver metal letters • 6 White ¾" diameter silk flowers • 20 gauge Silver wire (three 10", two 4") • Acrylic paint (Chocolate, Robin's egg) • Paintbrush • Wire cutters • Round-nose pliers • Red line tape • Adhesive

INSTRUCTIONS:

Paint edges only of chipboard square Blue. Paint all of chipboard heart Brown. Let dry. • Adhere Blue cardstock square to the front of the chipboard square. Tape metal letters and heart in place. Apply small rhinestones to heart and one medium in each corner of chipboard. • Fold the 4" wires in half and tape to the bottom back of chipboard square. • Using the 10" wires, make a small loop in one end of each with Round-nose pliers. Twirl into loose swirls using your fingers. Curl other ends around pencil. Tape wire swirls and silk flowers to top back of chipboard square. Apply rhinestones to centers of swirls. Tape the remaining cardstock square to hide the wires.

Initials Cake Topper

Initials are modern and very popular. These make an unusual cake topper.

SIZE: 9" wide x 7" tall

MATERIALS:

Cardstock (2 Brown 6" x 6") • Chipboard letters (one 5", two 3") • Blue rhinestones (10 large, 6 medium) • 2 Silver 20 gauge wires 4" long • Acrylic paint (Chocolate, Robin's egg) • Paintbrush • Wire cutters • Red line tape • Adhesive

INSTRUCTIONS:

Paint small chipboard letters Blue. Paint edges and back of large letter Brown. Let dry. • Cover the front of the large chipboard letter with Brown cardstock. • Fold each 4" wire in half. Attach to bottom back of the large letter with Red line tape. Cover the wires with a scrap of Brown cardstock. • Adhere small letters one each side of the large one. Apply 3 medium rhinestones to each small letter and large rhinestones to the large letter.

for the Reception

Giving Cone

Instead of a giving tree, make a giving cone. Guests can place their envelopes filled with money inside the cone for a wonderful memento.

SIZE: 5½" diameter, 12½" tall

MATERIALS:

12" paper mache cone • 13" x 17" White beaded paper • 2½" x 3½" Brown dot cardstock • 2' x 3" die cut tag • 14" pleated crepe paper • White shredded paper • 2½" x 3⅜" White butterfly • Rhinestones (8 Clear, 10 Blue) • Vintage button • Blue paper ½" diameter flower • Ribbon (21" Brown velvet ¼" wide, 12" Blue-Brown ⅛" wide) • 2 Silver ¼" eyelets • 8½" x 11" Clear adhesive transparency • *Tsukineko* Versamagic Sea Breeze inkpad • Light Blue acrylic paint • ¼" hole punch • Eyelet tools • Paintbrush • Red line tape • Adhesive

INSTRUCTIONS:

Paint inside and top edge of cone Light Blue. Let dry. • Wrap beaded paper around cone securing with adhesive as you go. Align paper at point and trim off excess around top when completely wrapped. Set eyelet in holes of cone for hanger. Tape crepe paper around the top of the cone. Thread Brown ribbon through eyelets and knot. • Apply 16 rhinestones around cone on crepe paper. Attach butterfly. Ink edges of tag. Adhere to Brown dot cardstock. • Computer print bride and groom names and date on Clear adhesive transparency. Cut to fit tag. Apply rhinestones to tag and flower center. Attach flower to tag. Attach ribbon to back of Brown dot cardstock. Tape to front of cone. Adhere vintage button to cone point.

Candy Popper

SIZE: 1¼" x 1¼" x 5½"

MATERIALS:

Candy • 6" x 6" Ivory print cardstock • 8½" x 11" Clear adhesive transparency • 12" Blue ½" wide ribbon • 4 Blue rhinestones • Die cuts (Blue tag, *AccuCut* Candy Popper) • *Tsukineko* Versamagic Sea Breeze inkpad • Adhesive

INSTRUCTIONS:

Die cut popper from Ivory print cardstock. Fold into shape. Fill with candy. Secure closed using adhesive. • Cut ribbon in half and knot on each end of the popper. • Computer print bride and groom names and wedding date on Clear adhesive transparency. Cut to fit tag. Ink tag edges. Let dry. Adhere tag to popper. Apply rhinestones to the tag.

Reception Favors

11

Presentation makes all the difference. Rhinestones and ribbon turn ordinary items into sparkling gifts and favors for appreciated guests.

Bag with Topper

SIZE: 2¾" x 4"

MATERIALS:
Candy • 2¾" x 8½" vellum • 2" x 3" Blue cardstock • 2" x 3½" plastic bag • Blue paper ½" flower • Clear tiny rhinestone • 6" Brown ⅜" wide ribbon • Circle word stamp • *Ranger* (Clear embossing powder, Heat it Craft Tool) • *Tsukineko* Jumbo Java Versamagic inkpad • Bone folder • Ruler • ¼" hole punch

INSTRUCTIONS:
Score vellum on long side at 3¾" and 4¾" using ruler and bone folder. Fold on scored lines. On one side of vellum, emboss word circle in Brown ink using Clear powder. Score Blue cardstock at 1" on short side. Fold on scored line to make topper. • Place candy in plastic bag. Center bag in between vellum sides. Place topper over vellum sides and punch 2 holes through all layers. Thread ribbon from front to back in holes. Then cross over and thread back to front. • Adhere flower to center of stamped circle. Apply rhinestone to flower center.

Wire Basket Favor

SIZE: 2½" x 3" x 3" tall

MATERIALS:
Peanuts • 2½" x 3" x 3" wire basket • 6" pleated White crepe paper 8" Blue velvet ⅜" wide ribbon • Blue paper 1" flower • Blue rhinestones (1 large, 10" strip of small stones) • Adhesive

INSTRUCTIONS:
Apply rhinestone strip around top rim of basket. Tie bow on handle. Adhere flower to bow. Adhere large Blue rhinestone to flower center. Insert crepe paper as liner in basket. Place peanuts in basket.

Bubbles Favor

SIZE: 2" diameter, 5" tall

MATERIALS:
8 oz bubbles bottle • Cardstock (3" x 7½" Brown dot, 1½" x 7½" Ivory stripe) • 8½" x 11" Clear adhesive transparency • 2 Blue rhinestones • Oval die cut label • Adhesive

INSTRUCTIONS:
Adhere Brown dot cardstock around the bubble container. Adhere stripe cardstock over it. Adhere oval label. • Computer print names of bride and groom and wedding date on Clear adhesive transparency. Cut out to fit the label. Apply rhinestones to label.

Round Silver Box

SIZE: 2½" diameter, ⅞" tall

MATERIALS:
2½" round plastic box • Candy kisses • 8½" x 11" White text paper • 17 Blue rhinestones

INSTRUCTIONS:
Computer print "hugs and kisses from bride and groom" on White paper. Cut to ⅝" x 2½" size. Place candy and paper in box and close. Apply rhinestones to top and sides of box.

Almond Bag

SIZE: 3" x 4"

MATERIALS:
3" x 4" White organza bag • Candy • 8½" x 11" White cardstock • Mr. & Mrs. rub-on • Blue paper 1" flower • Blue rhinestone • Tiny tag template • ⅛" hole punch • Adhesive

INSTRUCTIONS:
Apply rub-on to bag. Fill with almonds. Pull draw string on bag to close. • Computer print bride and groom names and wedding date on White cardstock. Trace tiny tag template over printed words and cut out. Punch hole in tag. Attach to string on bag. Tie a bow. Adhere flower to bow and rhinestone to flower.

12 Thank You... Special Cards!

Dandelion Card

Express your gratitude to those who shared your day and for all the wonderful gifts. Make your cards special.

SIZE: 4¼" x 5½"

MATERIALS:
4¼" x 5½" Green card • *Heidi Grace* (Cardstock: 2½" x 5½" Yellow Stripe, 3" x 3" White; Plastic shapes: Swirl, Flower) • 5½" Yellow ¼" wide ribbon • Clear rhinestone • Stamps (Thank you, *Heidi Grace* Swirl, Flower) • *Tsukineko* Versamagic (Thatched Straw inkpad, Embossing pad) • *Ranger* (Adirondack Bottle Green inkpad, Clear embossing powder, Heat it Craft Tool, Cut n' Dry sponge) • Foam tape • Adhesive

INSTRUCTIONS:
Stamp swirl on card using Versamark pad. • Ink the edges of the Yellow stripe cardstock with Bottle Green and adhere to card. Adhere ribbon and plastic swirls. Emboss flower on White cardstock using Clear powder and Thatched Straw ink. Cut out. Tape flower to card. Adhere plastic flower to stamped flower. Adhere rhinestone to center of plastic flower. Stamp 'thank you' in Bottle Green ink.